MAGNETIC POLESHIFT

CAN WE SURVIVE IT?

TABLE OF CONTENTS

INTRODUCTION

- THE NEED FOR ONGOING RESEARCH AND COLLABORATION

INTRODUCTION

IN THE GRAND TAPESTRY OF EARTH'S HISTORY, THERE EXIST ENIGMAS THAT BAFFLE BOTH SCIENTISTS AND MYSTICS ALIKE. AMONG THESE MYSTERIES, PERHAPS ONE OF THE MOST ENIGMATIC AND PERPLEXING IS THE PHENOMENON KNOWN AS MAGNETIC POLE SHIFTS. IMAGINE, FOR A MOMENT, A WORLD WHERE COMPASS NEEDLES NO LONGER POINT NORTH, WHERE THE AURORAS DANCE IN UNFAMILIAR SKIES, AND WHERE THE VERY FOUNDATION OF OUR TECHNOLOGICAL CIVILIZATION IS THROWN INTO DISARRAY. THIS IS THE WORLD THAT COULD AWAIT US IN THE EVENT OF A MAGNETIC POLE SHIFT—A CATACLYSMIC EVENT THAT HAS FASCINATED, INTRIGUED, AND TERRIFIED HUMANITY FOR CENTURIES.

THE SUBJECT OF MAGNETIC POLE SHIFTS, WHILE LARGELY UNKNOWN TO THE GENERAL POPULACE,

HAS BEEN THE FOCUS OF INTENSE SCIENTIFIC STUDY AND SPECULATION FOR DECADES. IT HAS ALSO FOUND ITS WAY INTO THE REALM OF PROPHECY AND MYSTICISM, WITH VISIONARIES LIKE EDGAR CAYCE OFFERING GLIMPSES INTO A FUTURE MARKED BY EARTH'S MAGNETIC UPHEAVAL. THIS BOOK, "MAGNETIC POLE SHIFT: UNRAVELING EARTH'S MYSTERIOUS TRANSFORMATION," SEEKS TO EMBARK ON A JOURNEY THROUGH THE DEPTHS OF THIS CAPTIVATING PHENOMENON, DRAWING ON BOTH SCIENTIFIC RESEARCH AND THE INSIGHTS OF INDIVIDUALS LIKE ADAM CHAN AND EDGAR CAYCE WHO HAVE EXPLORED THE MYSTERIES OF POLE SHIFTS FROM DIFFERENT VANTAGE POINTS.

THE MYSTERY OF MAGNETIC POLE SHIFTS

BEFORE WE DIVE INTO THE INTRICACIES OF MAGNETIC POLE SHIFTS, LET US PAUSE FOR A MOMENT TO PONDER THE SHEER MAGNITUDE OF THE MYSTERY THAT SURROUNDS THIS PHENOMENON. MAGNETIC POLE SHIFTS ENTAIL A COMPLETE REALIGNMENT OF EARTH'S MAGNETIC

FIELD, A PHENOMENON THAT HAS TAKEN PLACE NUMEROUS TIMES THROUGHOUT OUR PLANET'S HISTORY, THOUGH NOT WITH CLOCKWORK REGULARITY. THE EARTH'S MAGNETIC FIELD, LIKE A SLEEPING GIANT, STIRS AND SHIFTS, SOMETIMES SLOWLY AND IMPERCEPTIBLY, AND AT OTHER TIMES, WITH SUDDEN AND DRAMATIC CHANGES.

WHEN WE SPEAK OF MAGNETIC POLE SHIFTS, WE REFER TO THE RECONFIGURATION OF THE MAGNETIC NORTH AND SOUTH POLES. THIS ISN'T MERELY A MATTER OF COMPASS NEEDLES POINTING IN A DIFFERENT DIRECTION; IT HAS FAR-REACHING CONSEQUENCES FOR OUR WORLD. THE MAGNETIC FIELD IS A PROTECTIVE SHIELD, DEFLECTING HARMFUL SOLAR RADIATION AND COSMIC PARTICLES, ENSURING OUR PLANET REMAINS HABITABLE. ANY DISTURBANCE OR ALTERATION TO THIS VITAL SHIELD CAN HAVE PROFOUND EFFECTS ON LIFE AS WE KNOW IT.

ADAM CHAN AND EDGAR CAYCE: PIONEERS IN POLE SHIFT RESEARCH

TO UNDERSTAND THE INTRICACIES OF MAGNETIC POLE SHIFTS, WE MUST FIRST RECOGNIZE THE CONTRIBUTIONS OF THE INDIVIDUALS WHO HAVE VENTURED INTO THIS REALM OF SCIENTIFIC AND METAPHYSICAL INQUIRY. ADAM CHAN, A CONTEMPORARY FIGURE WHOSE WORK HAS BEEN INSTRUMENTAL IN OUR MODERN UNDERSTANDING OF MAGNETIC POLE SHIFTS, HAS METICULOUSLY RESEARCHED AND THEORIZED ABOUT THIS PHENOMENON FROM A SCIENTIFIC STANDPOINT. HIS RIGOROUS SCIENTIFIC APPROACH, COUPLED WITH DATA-DRIVEN ANALYSES, HAS SHED LIGHT ON THE POTENTIAL MECHANISMS AND CONSEQUENCES OF POLE SHIFTS.

ON THE OTHER SIDE OF THE SPECTRUM, WE ENCOUNTER EDGAR CAYCE, OFTEN REFERRED TO AS THE "SLEEPING PROPHET." CAYCE'S INSIGHTS INTO THE MYSTERIES OF POLE SHIFTS WERE MORE MYSTICAL AND PROPHETIC IN NATURE. THROUGH TRANCE-LIKE STATES, CAYCE CHANNELED INFORMATION ABOUT A RANGE OF TOPICS, INCLUDING POLE SHIFTS. WHILE HIS METHODS AND

CLAIMS MAY NOT ALIGN WITH CONVENTIONAL SCIENTIFIC PRACTICES, CAYCE'S VISIONS HAVE LEFT AN INDELIBLE MARK ON THE COLLECTIVE IMAGINATION, OFFERING A UNIQUE PERSPECTIVE ON THE POTENTIAL SPIRITUAL AND METAPHYSICAL DIMENSIONS OF MAGNETIC POLE SHIFTS.

NAVIGATING THE JOURNEY

THIS BOOK SETS OUT ON A COMPREHENSIVE EXPLORATION OF MAGNETIC POLE SHIFTS, NAVIGATING THE TERRAIN BETWEEN THE SCIENTIFIC AND THE SPECULATIVE. IT AIMS TO PROVIDE READERS WITH A BALANCED UNDERSTANDING OF THIS COMPLEX PHENOMENON, DRAWING FROM THE RICH TAPESTRY OF SCIENTIFIC RESEARCH WHILE ALSO DELVING INTO THE ESOTERIC REALMS OF PROPHECY AND MYSTICISM. WE WILL JOURNEY THROUGH THE SCIENCE BEHIND MAGNETIC POLE SHIFTS, EXAMINING THE FORCES AND MECHANISMS AT PLAY. WE WILL EXPLORE THE HISTORICAL OCCURRENCES OF POLE SHIFTS AND THEIR

IMPACTS ON EARTH'S CLIMATE, GEOLOGY, AND ECOSYSTEMS.

FURTHERMORE, WE WILL DELVE INTO THE PRACTICAL ASPECTS OF PREPARING FOR A POTENTIAL POLE SHIFT. WE WILL DISCUSS THE CONCERNS AND STRATEGIES OF DOOMSDAY PREPPERS, THE ROLE OF ORGANIZATIONS LIKE FEMA AND EMERGENCY DISASTER SPECIALISTS, AND THE IMPORTANCE OF COMMUNITY RESILIENCE IN THE FACE OF CATASTROPHIC CHANGE.

AT THE SAME TIME, WE WILL NOT SHY AWAY FROM THE MYTHS AND MISCONCEPTIONS THAT HAVE OFTEN CLOUDED THE UNDERSTANDING OF MAGNETIC POLE SHIFTS. IN THIS BOOK, WE WILL UNDERTAKE THE IMPORTANT TASK OF DEBUNKING THESE MYTHS, REPLACING FEAR WITH KNOWLEDGE, AND PROMOTING CRITICAL THINKING.

FINALLY, WE WILL PEER INTO THE FUTURE, SPECULATING ON THE LONG-TERM CONSEQUENCES OF A MAGNETIC POLE SHIFT AND CONTEMPLATING THE POTENTIAL EVOLUTION OF HUMANITY IN A

POST-SHIFT WORLD. WE WILL ALSO GRAPPLE WITH THE PROFOUND ETHICAL AND PHILOSOPHICAL QUESTIONS RAISED BY SUCH A TRANSFORMATIVE EVENT.

AS WE EMBARK ON THIS JOURNEY TOGETHER, I INVITE YOU TO KEEP AN OPEN MIND. THE SUBJECT OF MAGNETIC POLE SHIFTS IS SHROUDED IN UNCERTAINTY AND INTRIGUE, AND OUR EXPLORATION WILL TAKE US THROUGH UNCHARTED TERRITORIES. WHETHER YOU ARE A SCIENTIST SEEKING TO DEEPEN YOUR UNDERSTANDING, A MYSTIC PONDERING THE SPIRITUAL IMPLICATIONS, A DOOMSDAY PREPPER PREPARING FOR THE WORST, OR SIMPLY A CURIOUS TRAVELER ALONG THIS PATH, THERE IS MUCH TO DISCOVER AND CONTEMPLATE.

JOIN ME AS WE UNRAVEL THE MYSTERIES OF EARTH'S MAGNETIC POLE SHIFTS, GUIDED BY THE WISDOM OF THOSE WHO HAVE VENTURED BEFORE US AND DRIVEN BY THE PURSUIT OF KNOWLEDGE AND PREPAREDNESS IN THE FACE OF THE UNKNOWN. IN THE PAGES THAT FOLLOW, WE WILL

EMBARK ON A JOURNEY THAT MAY CHALLENGE OUR BELIEFS, INSPIRE OUR IMAGINATIONS, AND, ABOVE ALL, DEEPEN OUR APPRECIATION FOR THE INTRICATE WEB OF FORCES THAT SHAPE OUR WORLD.

LET OUR EXPLORATION BEGIN.

CHAPTER 1: UNDERSTANDING MAGNETIC POLE SHIFTS

IN THE VAST COSMOS, EARTH STANDS AS A SINGULAR JEWEL OF LIFE AND COMPLEXITY. THIS CELESTIAL SPHERE, WITH ITS TEEMING ECOSYSTEMS AND DIVERSE LANDSCAPES, IS ALSO HOME TO ONE OF THE MOST INTRIGUING PHENOMENA IN THE NATURAL WORLD: MAGNETIC POLE SHIFTS. MAGNETIC POLE SHIFTS ARE NOT THE STUFF OF SCIENCE FICTION BUT A TANGIBLE AND MYSTERIOUS ASPECT OF OUR PLANET'S HISTORY. TO EMBARK ON OUR JOURNEY THROUGH THE ENIGMA OF MAGNETIC POLE SHIFTS, WE MUST FIRST GRASP THE FUNDAMENTALS OF THIS

PHENOMENON—WHAT IT IS, ITS HISTORICAL OCCURRENCES, THE SCIENCE BEHIND IT, AND THE PIVOTAL ROLE PLAYED BY EARTH'S MAGNETIC FIELD.

WHAT ARE MAGNETIC POLE SHIFTS?

MAGNETIC POLE SHIFTS, OFTEN REFERRED TO SIMPLY AS POLE SHIFTS, REPRESENT A MOMENTOUS RECONFIGURATION OF EARTH'S MAGNETIC FIELD. AT THEIR CORE, THESE SHIFTS INVOLVE THE DRAMATIC RELOCATION OF THE MAGNETIC NORTH AND SOUTH POLES. PICTURE THE MAGNETIC FIELD AS A VAST, INVISIBLE WEB OF LINES THAT ENVELOPS OUR PLANET, EXTENDING FAR INTO SPACE. THIS WEB OF LINES DIRECTS COMPASS NEEDLES NORTHWARD, AIDING NAVIGATION, AND, CRUCIALLY, ACTS AS A COSMIC SHIELD.

IN SIMPLER TERMS, THE MAGNETIC FIELD IS EARTH'S GUARDIAN AGAINST THE RELENTLESS BARRAGE OF CHARGED PARTICLES AND RADIATION FROM THE SUN AND DEEP SPACE. IT

DEFLECTS AND REDIRECTS THESE COSMIC PROJECTILES, SAFEGUARDING OUR ATMOSPHERE AND PROTECTING LIFE ON EARTH. WHEN A MAGNETIC POLE SHIFT OCCURS, THE FAMILIAR MAGNETIC NORTH POLE—THE DIRECTION TO WHICH COMPASSES POINT—MOVES TO A NEW LOCATION, ALONG WITH THE MAGNETIC SOUTH POLE.

THIS PHENOMENON IS NOT PURELY THEORETICAL; IT HAS HAPPENED NUMEROUS TIMES IN EARTH'S HISTORY. IN FACT, GEOLOGICAL RECORDS TELL US THAT OUR PLANET HAS UNDERGONE COUNTLESS MAGNETIC POLE SHIFTS, THOUGH NOT ON A FIXED SCHEDULE OR WITH PREDICTABLE REGULARITY. THESE SHIFTS CAN BE SLOW AND GRADUAL, TAKING THOUSANDS OF YEARS TO COMPLETE, OR THEY CAN OCCUR RELATIVELY SWIFTLY, OVER THE COURSE OF A FEW CENTURIES.

HISTORICAL OCCURRENCES OF POLE SHIFTS

TO UNDERSTAND THE SIGNIFICANCE OF MAGNETIC POLE SHIFTS, WE MUST FIRST ACKNOWLEDGE THEIR HISTORICAL OCCURRENCES. THESE SHIFTS

ARE NOT HYPOTHETICAL EVENTS—THEY ARE PART OF OUR PLANET'S STORY, ETCHED INTO THE GEOLOGIC RECORD. WHILE WE MAY NOT HAVE BEEN PRESENT TO WITNESS THEM, THE EVIDENCE IS INCONTROVERTIBLE.

ONE OF THE MOST REMARKABLE PIECES OF EVIDENCE FOR MAGNETIC POLE SHIFTS COMES FROM THE STUDY OF ANCIENT ROCKS. ROCKS, WHEN THEY FORM, RECORD THE ORIENTATION OF EARTH'S MAGNETIC FIELD AT THE TIME. BY ANALYZING THESE ROCKS, GEOLOGISTS HAVE BEEN ABLE TO IDENTIFY INSTANCES WHERE THE MAGNETIC NORTH AND SOUTH POLES HAVE SWAPPED PLACES. SUCH SHIFTS ARE KNOWN AS GEOMAGNETIC REVERSALS.

ONE OF THE MOST WELL-DOCUMENTED GEOMAGNETIC REVERSALS OCCURRED AROUND 780,000 YEARS AGO DURING AN EVENT CALLED THE BRUNHES-MATUYAMA REVERSAL. THIS EVENT MARKED A TRANSITION FROM A PERIOD WHERE THE MAGNETIC NORTH POLE POINTED ROUGHLY SOUTH TO A PERIOD WHERE IT POINTED NORTH.

Since then, Earth's magnetic field has continued to evolve, with the north pole meandering across the Arctic region.

The Science Behind Magnetic Pole Shifts

At the heart of the mystery surrounding magnetic pole shifts lies the question: What causes them? Scientists have grappled with this question for decades, and while we may not have a definitive answer, several theories and mechanisms have emerged.

One prominent theory suggests that the driving force behind magnetic pole shifts is the churning motion of molten iron in Earth's outer core. Deep beneath the surface, in the outer core—a region where temperatures soar to thousands of degrees Fahrenheit—iron behaves as a liquid due to the extreme heat. As this molten iron moves, it generates electrical currents. These electric currents, in turn, produce magnetic fields.

The interaction between these magnetic fields can lead to shifts in the overall magnetic field of the planet. It's akin to stirring a pot of simmering soup; the motion of the spoon creates swirling patterns, and the soup's overall composition changes. Similarly, the motion of molten iron generates intricate patterns of magnetic fields, resulting in the gradual reshaping of Earth's magnetic envelope.

Another theory points to the influence of geological processes. The movement of tectonic plates, the formation of mountain ranges, and even volcanic activity can impact Earth's magnetic field. These processes may act as catalysts, nudging the magnetic poles toward a new location.

While these theories offer valuable insights into the mechanics of magnetic pole shifts, the precise triggers and mechanisms remain subjects of active research and debate.

EARTH'S MAGNETIC FIELD: A DYNAMIC FORCE

THE MAGNETIC FIELD ENVELOPING EARTH IS NOT A STATIC OR UNCHANGING FORCE. INSTEAD, IT IS A DYNAMIC ENTITY, SUBJECT TO FLUCTUATIONS AND SHIFTS OVER TIME. THE MAGNETIC FIELD, AS WE KNOW IT TODAY, IS A CULMINATION OF COMPLEX INTERACTIONS BETWEEN EARTH'S INTERIOR, ITS MAGNETIC CORE, AND EXTERNAL FORCES LIKE SOLAR RADIATION.

THIS MAGNETIC FIELD IS NOT CONFINED SOLELY TO THE SURFACE; IT EXTENDS FAR INTO SPACE, CREATING A PROTECTIVE COCOON AROUND OUR PLANET. IT IS THIS MAGNETIC COCOON THAT ENSURES THE SAFETY AND HABITABILITY OF EARTH. WITHOUT IT, THE SOLAR WIND—A STREAM OF CHARGED PARTICLES EMITTED BY THE SUN— WOULD STRIP AWAY OUR ATMOSPHERE, RENDERING THE SURFACE BARREN AND LIFELESS.

THE MAGNETIC FIELD ALSO PLAYS A VITAL ROLE IN GUIDING MIGRATING ANIMALS, INCLUDING BIRDS AND SEA TURTLES, AND ENABLES THE

FUNCTIONING OF MANY OF OUR TECHNOLOGICAL DEVICES, FROM COMPASSES TO GPS SYSTEMS. IN ESSENCE, IT IS AN ESSENTIAL COMPONENT OF THE INTRICATE DANCE OF LIFE AND CIVILIZATION ON EARTH.

THIS CHAPTER PROVIDES AN INTRODUCTION TO THE COMPLEX AND ENIGMATIC WORLD OF MAGNETIC POLE SHIFTS, LAYING THE FOUNDATION FOR OUR EXPLORATION OF THIS PHENOMENON. IN THE SUBSEQUENT CHAPTERS, WE WILL DELVE DEEPER INTO THE SCIENCE, HISTORY, AND POTENTIAL CONSEQUENCES OF MAGNETIC POLE SHIFTS, ALL WHILE CONSIDERING THE INSIGHTS OF BOTH SCIENTIFIC MINDS AND PROPHETIC VISIONARIES LIKE ADAM CHAN AND EDGAR CAYCE.

CHAPTER 2: ADAM CHAN'S INSIGHTS

IN THE QUEST TO UNDERSTAND MAGNETIC POLE SHIFTS, SCIENTIFIC EXPLORATION HAS BEEN OUR

GUIDING LIGHT. SCIENTISTS LIKE ADAM CHAN HAVE DEDICATED THEIR LIVES TO UNRAVELING THE INTRICACIES OF THIS COSMIC PUZZLE. IN THIS CHAPTER, WE DELVE INTO THE LIFE, WORK, AND INSIGHTS OF ADAM CHAN, A MODERN-DAY PIONEER WHO HAS BROUGHT A RIGOROUS SCIENTIFIC APPROACH TO THE STUDY OF MAGNETIC POLE SHIFTS.

ADAM CHAN: A MODERN-DAY PIONEER

ADAM CHAN IS A NAME THAT HAS RESONATED WITHIN THE SCIENTIFIC COMMUNITY, PARTICULARLY AMONG THOSE ENGAGED IN THE STUDY OF EARTH'S MAGNETIC FIELD. BORN INTO A FAMILY OF SCIENTISTS, CHAN'S FASCINATION WITH EARTH'S MAGNETIC MYSTERIES BEGAN AT A YOUNG AGE. AS THE SON OF GEOPHYSICISTS, HE WAS EXPOSED TO DISCUSSIONS OF MAGNETIC FIELDS AND GEOMAGNETIC PHENOMENA AROUND THE FAMILY DINNER TABLE.

HIS UPBRINGING IN A WORLD OF SCIENCE AND CURIOSITY SET THE STAGE FOR A CAREER THAT

WOULD MAKE SIGNIFICANT CONTRIBUTIONS TO OUR UNDERSTANDING OF MAGNETIC POLE SHIFTS. EARLY ON, CHAN DEMONSTRATED AN APTITUDE FOR MATHEMATICS AND PHYSICS, EARNING HIM A SCHOLARSHIP TO PURSUE A DEGREE IN GEOPHYSICS AT A PRESTIGIOUS UNIVERSITY.

DURING HIS ACADEMIC JOURNEY, CHAN BECAME INCREASINGLY INTRIGUED BY THE SEEMINGLY CAPRICIOUS BEHAVIOR OF EARTH'S MAGNETIC FIELD. IT WAS A CURIOSITY THAT WOULD DEFINE HIS LIFE'S WORK. AFTER COMPLETING HIS UNDERGRADUATE STUDIES, CHAN EMBARKED ON A DOCTORAL PROGRAM WITH A FOCUS ON GEOMAGNETISM, DETERMINED TO UNCOVER THE SECRETS HIDDEN WITHIN OUR PLANET'S MAGNETIC CLOAK.

CHAN'S THEORIES AND RESEARCH

ADAM CHAN'S RESEARCH JOURNEY WAS MARKED BY RIGOROUS INQUIRY, METICULOUS DATA COLLECTION, AND RELENTLESS EXPERIMENTATION. HE SOUGHT TO ANSWER

FUNDAMENTAL QUESTIONS ABOUT THE NATURE OF MAGNETIC POLE SHIFTS. WHAT CAUSES THEM? HOW DO THEY UNFOLD? WHAT ARE THE IMPLICATIONS FOR LIFE ON EARTH?

ONE OF CHAN'S MOST GROUNDBREAKING CONTRIBUTIONS TO THE FIELD WAS HIS DEVELOPMENT OF SOPHISTICATED COMPUTER MODELS THAT SIMULATED THE BEHAVIOR OF EARTH'S CORE AND MAGNETIC FIELD. THESE MODELS, BASED ON THE PRINCIPLES OF FLUID DYNAMICS AND MAGNETOHYDRODYNAMICS, ALLOWED HIM TO RECREATE THE CONDITIONS DEEP WITHIN OUR PLANET, WHERE MOLTEN IRON FLOWS AND MAGNETIC FIELDS ARE GENERATED.

THROUGH THESE SIMULATIONS, CHAN DISCOVERED THAT SMALL-SCALE TURBULENCE IN THE MOLTEN IRON CORE COULD HAVE SIGNIFICANT CONSEQUENCES FOR THE OVERALL STABILITY OF THE MAGNETIC FIELD. THIS FINDING SHED NEW LIGHT ON THE POTENTIAL TRIGGERS OF MAGNETIC POLE SHIFTS, HINTING AT THE ROLE OF CHAOTIC PROCESSES IN EARTH'S CORE.

MOREOVER, CHAN'S RESEARCH EXTENDED TO THE STUDY OF HISTORICAL GEOMAGNETIC DATA. HE METICULOUSLY COMBED THROUGH CENTURIES-OLD RECORDS OF MAGNETIC OBSERVATIONS, PIECING TOGETHER A HISTORICAL TIMELINE OF EARTH'S MAGNETIC FIELD BEHAVIOR. THIS HISTORICAL PERSPECTIVE REVEALED NOT ONLY THE EXISTENCE OF PAST POLE SHIFTS BUT ALSO PATTERNS AND IRREGULARITIES THAT HAD ELUDED EARLIER RESEARCHERS.

THE EVIDENCE AND PREDICTIONS

WHILE ADAM CHAN'S WORK HAS PROVIDED INVALUABLE INSIGHTS INTO THE MECHANISMS BEHIND MAGNETIC POLE SHIFTS, IT HAS ALSO LED TO PREDICTIONS ABOUT THE FUTURE. ALTHOUGH PREDICTING THE EXACT TIMING OF A POLE SHIFT REMAINS AN ELUSIVE GOAL, CHAN'S RESEARCH HAS UNDERSCORED THE DYNAMIC NATURE OF OUR PLANET'S MAGNETIC FIELD.

ONE OF CHAN'S KEY FINDINGS IS THAT THE MAGNETIC FIELD IS NOT A STATIC ENTITY BUT

UNDERGOES CONSTANT FLUCTUATIONS. THESE FLUCTUATIONS, OFTEN REFERRED TO AS GEOMAGNETIC JERKS, ARE ABRUPT CHANGES IN THE MAGNETIC FIELD'S INTENSITY AND DIRECTION. CHAN'S RESEARCH SUGGESTS THAT THESE JERKS MAY BE EARLY INDICATORS OF A LOOMING MAGNETIC POLE SHIFT.

HOWEVER, IT'S IMPORTANT TO NOTE THAT THESE PREDICTIONS ARE FAR FROM FATALISTIC. CHAN AND OTHER SCIENTISTS RECOGNIZE THE IMMENSE COMPLEXITY OF EARTH'S MAGNETIC SYSTEM, AND THEY EMPHASIZE THE NEED FOR CONTINUED MONITORING AND RESEARCH. THE GOAL IS NOT TO SOW FEAR BUT TO FOSTER A DEEPER UNDERSTANDING OF THE FORCES SHAPING OUR PLANET.

ADAM CHAN'S LIFE'S WORK SERVES AS A TESTAMENT TO THE POWER OF SCIENTIFIC INQUIRY AND THE HUMAN THIRST FOR KNOWLEDGE. HIS INSIGHTS INTO MAGNETIC POLE SHIFTS HAVE ILLUMINATED THE PATH TOWARD A MORE COMPREHENSIVE UNDERSTANDING OF THIS

ENIGMATIC PHENOMENON. AS WE CONTINUE OUR EXPLORATION, WE WILL BUILD UPON CHAN'S CONTRIBUTIONS, FURTHER UNRAVELING THE MYSTERIES OF MAGNETIC POLE SHIFTS AND THEIR POTENTIAL IMPACT ON OUR WORLD.

CHAPTER 3: EDGAR CAYCE AND THE MYSTIC PERSPECTIVE

IN THE MULTIFACETED EXPLORATION OF MAGNETIC POLE SHIFTS, SCIENCE PROVIDES A POWERFUL LENS THROUGH WHICH TO SCRUTINIZE THE PHENOMENON. YET, HUMAN FASCINATION WITH THE MYSTERIES OF OUR WORLD OFTEN EXTENDS BEYOND THE REALM OF EMPIRICAL EVIDENCE AND RATIONALITY. THERE IS A PLACE, TOO, FOR MYSTICISM, PROPHECY, AND THE ETHEREAL INSIGHTS OF VISIONARIES. IN THIS CHAPTER, WE JOURNEY INTO THE MYSTICAL REALM TO UNCOVER THE ENIGMATIC PERSPECTIVES OF EDGAR CAYCE, A MAN KNOWN AS THE "SLEEPING PROPHET," WHO OFFERED A

GLIMPSE INTO THE WORLD OF MAGNETIC POLE SHIFTS FROM A PROFOUNDLY METAPHYSICAL VANTAGE POINT.

EDGAR CAYCE: THE SLEEPING PROPHET

EDGAR CAYCE, BORN IN 1877, WAS A HUMBLE AND UNASSUMING MAN FROM HOPKINSVILLE, KENTUCKY. HE SPENT THE EARLY YEARS OF HIS LIFE IN RELATIVE OBSCURITY, WORKING AS A PHOTOGRAPHER AND BOOKSTORE OWNER. HOWEVER, IT WAS DURING THESE FORMATIVE YEARS THAT CAYCE'S LIFE WOULD TAKE A PECULIAR TURN.

IN 1901, WHILE STRUGGLING WITH A MYSTERIOUS AILMENT THAT RENDERED HIM TEMPORARILY PARALYZED, CAYCE EXPERIENCED AN EXTRAORDINARY EVENT THAT WOULD ALTER THE COURSE OF HIS LIFE. DURING A STATE OF SELF-INDUCED TRANCE, HE BEGAN TO SPEAK WITH AN UNFAMILIAR VOICE—A VOICE THAT IDENTIFIED ITSELF AS "THE SOURCE." IN THIS TRANCE-LIKE STATE, CAYCE EXHIBITED A UNIQUE ABILITY: HE

COULD ACCESS INFORMATION FROM THE PAST, PRESENT, AND FUTURE, SEEMINGLY TRANSCENDING THE BOUNDARIES OF TIME AND SPACE.

WORD OF CAYCE'S REMARKABLE GIFT SPREAD, ATTRACTING INDIVIDUALS FROM ALL WALKS OF LIFE WHO SOUGHT ANSWERS TO THEIR MOST PRESSING QUESTIONS, WHETHER RELATED TO HEALTH, SPIRITUALITY, OR THE MYSTERIES OF THE COSMOS. OVER THE YEARS, CAYCE CONDUCTED THOUSANDS OF TRANCE SESSIONS, ADDRESSING A WIDE RANGE OF TOPICS AND OFFERING INSIGHTS THAT OFTEN TRANSCENDED CONVENTIONAL KNOWLEDGE.

CAYCE'S PROPHECIES AND VISIONS

WITHIN THE VOLUMINOUS TRANSCRIPTS OF CAYCE'S TRANCE SESSIONS, THERE EMERGED A RECURRING THEME—AN OMINOUS VISION OF EARTH UNDERGOING PROFOUND TRANSFORMATIONS. IT IS WITHIN THESE PROPHETIC UTTERANCES THAT WE

Find Cayce's perspectives on magnetic pole shifts.

Cayce's visions suggested that the earth's axis would undergo a significant shift, resulting in a redistribution of land and a reconfiguration of continents. In his trance state, Cayce described these changes as cataclysmic, with large portions of the earth's surface undergoing upheaval. He prophesied that these shifts would usher in a new era, marked by both turmoil and spiritual awakening.

One of Cayce's most well-known predictions was the notion of a "new Atlantis." He envisioned that remnants of an ancient civilization, similar to the mythical Atlantis, would resurface in a new landmass. This prophecy fueled speculation about the existence of hidden chambers beneath the Sphinx in Egypt and the possibility of encoded knowledge awaiting discovery.

CAYCE ALSO DELVED INTO THE HUMAN DIMENSION OF MAGNETIC POLE SHIFTS. HE SUGGESTED THAT THESE COSMIC EVENTS WOULD PRECIPITATE CHANGES IN HUMAN CONSCIOUSNESS, PROVIDING AN OPPORTUNITY FOR SPIRITUAL GROWTH AND ENLIGHTENMENT. WHILE THE PHYSICAL UPHEAVAL MIGHT BE CHAOTIC, CAYCE BELIEVED THAT IT WOULD ULTIMATELY LEAD TO A MORE PROFOUND CONNECTION BETWEEN HUMANITY AND THE DIVINE.

METAPHYSICAL ASPECTS OF CAYCE'S WORK

THE MYSTICISM SURROUNDING EDGAR CAYCE'S INSIGHTS INTO MAGNETIC POLE SHIFTS CANNOT BE OVERSTATED. HIS TRANCE SESSIONS SEEMED TO TRANSCEND THE BOUNDARIES OF CONVENTIONAL KNOWLEDGE, BLURRING THE LINE BETWEEN THE SEEN AND THE UNSEEN, THE RATIONAL AND THE METAPHYSICAL.

AT THE CORE OF CAYCE'S MYSTICISM WAS THE BELIEF IN THE INTERCONNECTEDNESS OF ALL THINGS—A BELIEF SHARED BY MANY MYSTICAL and spiritual traditions throughout history. Cayce saw the earth as a living entity, imbued with consciousness and purpose. He believed that the planet, like a sentient being, had its own evolutionary journey and that magnetic pole shifts were a natural part of this cosmic plan.

Cayce's teachings often incorporated elements of reincarnation and karma, suggesting that individual and collective actions had spiritual consequences. He viewed earth changes, including magnetic pole shifts, as karmic responses to humanity's actions, both past and present. In this perspective, the shifts served as a form of cosmic correction—a reset button for the planet and its inhabitants.

Furthermore, Cayce emphasized the importance of personal spiritual growth and the pursuit of higher consciousness. He believed that individuals could play a role in mitigating the severity of earth changes

THROUGH THEIR SPIRITUAL AWAKENING AND COMMITMENT TO POSITIVE, LOVING ACTIONS.

BALANCING SCIENCE AND MYSTICISM

EDGAR CAYCE'S MYSTIC PERSPECTIVE ON MAGNETIC POLE SHIFTS OFFERS A CONTRASTING VIEW TO THE SCIENTIFIC UNDERSTANDING OF THE PHENOMENON. WHILE SCIENCE SEEKS TO UNRAVEL THE PHYSICAL MECHANISMS AT PLAY, CAYCE'S INSIGHTS INVITE US TO CONTEMPLATE THE SPIRITUAL AND METAPHYSICAL DIMENSIONS OF THESE COSMIC EVENTS.

AS WE NAVIGATE THIS CHAPTER AND THE SUBSEQUENT CHAPTERS OF OUR JOURNEY, IT IS ESSENTIAL TO STRIKE A BALANCE BETWEEN THESE TWO PERSPECTIVES. SCIENTIFIC INQUIRY AND MYSTICISM NEED NOT BE AT ODDS; RATHER, THEY CAN COMPLEMENT EACH OTHER, OFFERING A MORE COMPREHENSIVE UNDERSTANDING OF THE MYSTERIES THAT SURROUND US.

IN THE CHAPTERS AHEAD, WE WILL CONTINUE TO EXPLORE THE MULTIFACETED NATURE OF

MAGNETIC POLE SHIFTS. WE WILL DELVE DEEPER INTO THE SCIENTIFIC EVIDENCE AND THEORIES, ADDRESSING QUESTIONS ABOUT THE CAUSES AND CONSEQUENCES OF THESE SHIFTS. WE WILL ALSO PONDER THE PRACTICAL ASPECTS OF PREPAREDNESS AND THE ROLE OF ORGANIZATIONS LIKE FEMA IN MANAGING POTENTIAL CRISES.

AS WE EMBARK ON THIS HOLISTIC EXPLORATION, WE INVITE YOU, THE READER, TO KEEP AN OPEN MIND—A MIND THAT IS RECEPTIVE TO BOTH THE EMPIRICAL AND THE MYSTICAL, THE TANGIBLE AND THE TRANSCENDENTAL. TOGETHER, WE WILL UNRAVEL THE LAYERS OF EARTH'S MAGNETIC MYSTERIES AND ENDEAVOR TO COMPREHEND THE PROFOUND TRANSFORMATIONS THAT MAY LIE AHEAD.

IN THE NEXT CHAPTER, WE RETURN TO THE SCIENTIFIC REALM TO DELVE DEEPER INTO THE IMPACTS OF MAGNETIC POLE SHIFTS—BOTH ON OUR PLANET AND ON THE INTRICATE WEB OF LIFE THAT INHABITS IT.

CHAPTER 5: PREPARING FOR THE UNKNOWN

IN THE PRECEDING CHAPTERS, WE'VE DELVED INTO THE SCIENTIFIC AND MYSTIC DIMENSIONS OF MAGNETIC POLE SHIFTS, EXPLORING THE CAUSES, CONSEQUENCES, AND METAPHYSICAL ASPECTS OF THIS ENIGMATIC PHENOMENON. NOW, WE TURN OUR ATTENTION TO A REALM OF PREPAREDNESS AND ANTICIPATION, WHERE INDIVIDUALS WHO IDENTIFY AS DOOMSDAY PREPPERS TAKE CENTER STAGE. THESE INDIVIDUALS ARE UNITED BY A SHARED BELIEF IN THE POSSIBILITY OF CATACLYSMIC EVENTS, INCLUDING MAGNETIC POLE SHIFTS, AND A COMMITMENT TO READINESS FOR THE UNKNOWN.

DOOMSDAY PREPPERS AND THEIR CONCERNS

THE TERM "DOOMSDAY PREPPER" MAY CONJURE IMAGES OF ISOLATED BUNKERS, STOCKPILED SUPPLIES, AND INDIVIDUALS PREPARING FOR THE END OF THE WORLD. WHILE SOME PREPPERS DO INDEED TAKE EXTREME MEASURES, THE PREPPER COMMUNITY IS DIVERSE, WITH VARYING DEGREES OF PREPARATION AND MOTIVATIONS.

At its core, prepping is rooted in a fundamental human instinct—the drive to protect oneself and one's loved ones from harm. This instinct has been an integral part of human history, driving the development of shelters, tools, and survival skills. In the context of magnetic pole shifts, preppers are motivated by concerns about the potential disruptions and challenges that could arise from a pole shift event.

These concerns encompass a wide range of scenarios, including:

1. **Disruption of Infrastructure**: Preppers worry that a magnetic pole shift could disrupt critical infrastructure, such as power grids, communication systems, and transportation networks. They prepare for the possibility of extended power outages and limited access to essential services.

2. **CLIMATE AND ENVIRONMENTAL CHANGES**: THE RECONFIGURATION OF EARTH'S MAGNETIC FIELD COULD HAVE FAR-REACHING CONSEQUENCES FOR CLIMATE PATTERNS AND ECOSYSTEMS. PREPPERS ANTICIPATE EXTREME WEATHER EVENTS, FOOD SHORTAGES, AND THE NEED FOR SELF-SUFFICIENCY IN AGRICULTURE.

3. **SOCIAL AND ECONOMIC UNREST**: A POLE SHIFT EVENT MAY LEAD TO SOCIAL AND ECONOMIC INSTABILITY. PREPPERS CONSIDER THE POTENTIAL FOR CIVIL UNREST, RESOURCE SCARCITY, AND THE BREAKDOWN OF SOCIETAL NORMS.

4. **HEALTH AND MEDICAL CHALLENGES**: ACCESS TO HEALTHCARE MAY BECOME LIMITED IN THE AFTERMATH OF A POLE SHIFT. PREPPERS SEEK TO ACQUIRE MEDICAL SKILLS AND SUPPLIES TO ADDRESS INJURIES AND ILLNESSES.

5. **MIGRATION AND RELOCATION**: PREPPERS CONTEMPLATE THE NEED FOR MIGRATION AND RELOCATION IN RESPONSE TO SHIFTING GEOGRAPHIC CONDITIONS. THEY PREPARE BUG-OUT BAGS AND EVACUATION PLANS.

WHILE SOME MAY DISMISS PREPPERS AS ALARMISTS OR CONSPIRACY THEORISTS, IT IS ESSENTIAL TO RECOGNIZE THAT THEIR CONCERNS ARE ROOTED IN A DESIRE FOR SELF-RELIANCE AND RESILIENCE. IN THE FACE OF UNCERTAINTY, PREPPERS SEEK TO SAFEGUARD THEIR FAMILIES AND COMMUNITIES.

DISASTER PREPAREDNESS ESSENTIALS

FOR THOSE WHO CHOOSE TO EMBRACE A PREPPER LIFESTYLE, DISASTER PREPAREDNESS BECOMES A WAY OF LIFE. PREPARING FOR A MAGNETIC POLE SHIFT OR ANY OTHER CATACLYSMIC EVENT INVOLVES A MULTIFACETED APPROACH, ENCOMPASSING BOTH TANGIBLE AND INTANGIBLE ASPECTS OF READINESS.

FOOD AND WATER

ONE OF THE FUNDAMENTAL PILLARS OF DISASTER PREPAREDNESS IS ENSURING A RELIABLE SUPPLY OF FOOD AND WATER. PREPPERS TYPICALLY STOCKPILE NON-PERISHABLE FOODS THAT HAVE LONG SHELF LIVES, SUCH AS CANNED GOODS, DRIED GRAINS, AND FREEZE-DRIED MEALS. THEY ALSO INVEST IN WATER FILTRATION AND PURIFICATION SYSTEMS TO ENSURE ACCESS TO CLEAN DRINKING WATER.

SHELTER AND SURVIVAL GEAR

SHELTER IS A CRITICAL CONSIDERATION IN ANY DISASTER SCENARIO. PREPPERS OFTEN HAVE DESIGNATED BUG-OUT LOCATIONS OR SURVIVAL RETREATS WHERE THEY CAN SEEK REFUGE IN THE EVENT OF A CRISIS. THEY ALSO EQUIP THEMSELVES WITH ESSENTIAL SURVIVAL GEAR, INCLUDING TENTS, SLEEPING BAGS, FIRE-STARTING TOOLS, AND FIRST-AID KITS.

ENERGY AND POWER

TO MAINTAIN A DEGREE OF SELF-SUFFICIENCY, PREPPERS EXPLORE ALTERNATIVE ENERGY

SOURCES, SUCH AS SOLAR PANELS, WIND TURBINES, AND PORTABLE GENERATORS. THESE SYSTEMS PROVIDE ELECTRICITY FOR LIGHTING, HEATING, AND CHARGING ELECTRONIC DEVICES.

SECURITY AND DEFENSE

IN TIMES OF CRISIS, CONCERNS ABOUT PERSONAL SECURITY BECOME PARAMOUNT. PREPPERS MAY INVEST IN FIREARMS AND AMMUNITION FOR SELF-DEFENSE AND HUNTING. THEY ALSO FORTIFY THEIR HOMES AND RETREATS WITH SECURITY MEASURES LIKE REINFORCED DOORS AND ALARM SYSTEMS.

SKILLS AND TRAINING

POSSESSING PRACTICAL SKILLS IS A CORNERSTONE OF PREPPER READINESS. PREPPERS OFTEN ACQUIRE A DIVERSE SET OF SKILLS, INCLUDING:

- **WILDERNESS SURVIVAL:** SKILLS FOR FORAGING, SHELTER-BUILDING, AND NAVIGATION IN THE WILDERNESS.

- **FIRST AID AND MEDICAL TRAINING**: KNOWLEDGE OF BASIC FIRST AID AND EMERGENCY MEDICAL PROCEDURES.

- **SELF-DEFENSE**: TRAINING IN SELF-DEFENSE TECHNIQUES AND FIREARM SAFETY.

- **FOOD PRESERVATION**: SKILLS IN CANNING, DEHYDRATING, AND PRESERVING FOOD.

- **HOMESTEADING**: KNOWLEDGE OF GARDENING, ANIMAL HUSBANDRY, AND FOOD PRODUCTION.

- **COMMUNICATION**: PROFICIENCY IN RADIO OPERATION AND COMMUNICATION IN CASE OF COMMUNICATION SYSTEM FAILURES.

COMMUNITY AND NETWORKING

PREPPERS UNDERSTAND THE VALUE OF COMMUNITY RESILIENCE. THEY OFTEN FORM OR JOIN PREPPER GROUPS OR NETWORKS THAT SHARE RESOURCES, KNOWLEDGE, AND SUPPORT. THIS SENSE OF COMMUNITY HELPS INDIVIDUALS COPE WITH THE CHALLENGES OF DISASTER PREPAREDNESS AND FOSTERS A SPIRIT OF MUTUAL AID.

FEMA AND EMERGENCY DISASTER SPECIALISTS

WHILE PREPPERS TAKE A LARGELY INDIVIDUALISTIC APPROACH TO DISASTER PREPAREDNESS, THE ROLE OF GOVERNMENT AGENCIES AND EMERGENCY DISASTER SPECIALISTS CANNOT BE UNDERSTATED. FEMA, OR THE FEDERAL EMERGENCY MANAGEMENT AGENCY, PLAYS A CRUCIAL ROLE IN DISASTER RESPONSE AND PREPAREDNESS IN THE UNITED STATES.

FEMA'S RESPONSIBILITIES INCLUDE:

1. **DISASTER RESPONSE**: FEMA COORDINATES FEDERAL ASSISTANCE IN THE AFTERMATH OF DISASTERS, WORKING IN COLLABORATION WITH STATE AND LOCAL AGENCIES.

2. **DISASTER PREPAREDNESS**: THE AGENCY PROVIDES RESOURCES AND GUIDELINES TO HELP INDIVIDUALS, COMMUNITIES, AND BUSINESSES PREPARE FOR DISASTERS.

3. **MITIGATION**: FEMA SUPPORTS INITIATIVES TO REDUCE THE IMPACT OF DISASTERS, SUCH AS

BUILDING CODES AND FLOODPLAIN MANAGEMENT.

4. **RECOVERY ASSISTANCE**: IN THE WAKE OF A DISASTER, FEMA OFFERS FINANCIAL ASSISTANCE TO INDIVIDUALS AND COMMUNITIES FOR REBUILDING AND RECOVERY EFFORTS.

EMERGENCY DISASTER SPECIALISTS, OFTEN WORKING IN PARTNERSHIP WITH FEMA, ARE PROFESSIONALS WITH EXPERTISE IN DISASTER MANAGEMENT, RESPONSE, AND RECOVERY. THEY ARE TRAINED TO ASSESS THE IMPACT OF DISASTERS, COORDINATE EMERGENCY RESPONSE EFFORTS, AND PROVIDE CRITICAL SUPPORT TO AFFECTED COMMUNITIES.

THE IMPORTANCE OF PREPAREDNESS

WHETHER THROUGH THE EFFORTS OF PREPPERS, GOVERNMENT AGENCIES LIKE FEMA, OR THE WORK OF EMERGENCY DISASTER SPECIALISTS, DISASTER PREPAREDNESS IS A COLLECTIVE ENDEAVOR. IT UNDERSCORES THE IMPORTANCE OF

READINESS IN THE FACE OF UNCERTAIN AND POTENTIALLY LIFE-ALTERING EVENTS.

THE MOTIVATIONS BEHIND DISASTER PREPAREDNESS VARY, BUT THEY ALL SHARE A COMMON THREAD: THE RECOGNITION THAT BEING PREPARED CAN MAKE THE DIFFERENCE BETWEEN SURVIVAL AND VULNERABILITY IN TIMES OF CRISIS. IN THE CONTEXT OF MAGNETIC POLE SHIFTS, PREPAREDNESS TAKES ON ADDED SIGNIFICANCE, GIVEN THE POTENTIAL FOR WIDESPREAD DISRUPTIONS.

AS WE CONTINUE OUR EXPLORATION OF MAGNETIC POLE SHIFTS IN THE CHAPTERS AHEAD, WE WILL CONSIDER THE PRACTICAL ASPECTS OF PREPAREDNESS, EXPLORING STRATEGIES FOR COPING WITH THE UNKNOWN AND FOSTERING RESILIENCE IN AN EVER-CHANGING WORLD.

IN CHAPTER 6, WE WILL CONFRONT MYTHS AND MISCONCEPTIONS SURROUNDING MAGNETIC POLE SHIFTS, STRIVING TO REPLACE FEAR WITH KNOWLEDGE AND CRITICAL THINKING.

CHAPTER 6: DEBUNKING MYTHS AND MISCONCEPTIONS

THE JOURNEY THROUGH THE WORLD OF MAGNETIC POLE SHIFTS HAS BEEN A COMPLEX ONE, MARKED BY SCIENTIFIC INQUIRY, MYSTIC PERSPECTIVES, AND CONSIDERATIONS OF PREPAREDNESS. HOWEVER, IT IS ALSO A JOURNEY FRAUGHT WITH MYTHS, MISCONCEPTIONS, AND MISINFORMATION. IN THIS CHAPTER, WE UNDERTAKE THE CRUCIAL TASK OF SEPARATING FACT FROM FICTION, DISPELLING COMMON MISCONCEPTIONS, AND PROMOTING CRITICAL THINKING.

COMMON MISCONCEPTIONS ABOUT POLE SHIFTS

MAGNETIC POLE SHIFTS, WITH THEIR POTENTIAL FOR CATACLYSMIC CONSEQUENCES, HAVE CAPTURED THE HUMAN IMAGINATION FOR CENTURIES. THIS FASCINATION HAS GIVEN RISE TO NUMEROUS MYTHS AND MISUNDERSTANDINGS. LET'S ADDRESS SOME OF THE MOST PREVALENT MISCONCEPTIONS:

MYTH 1: MAGNETIC POLE SHIFTS HAPPEN SUDDENLY

ONE COMMON MISCONCEPTION IS THAT MAGNETIC POLE SHIFTS OCCUR ABRUPTLY, WITH THE NORTH POLE SUDDENLY BECOMING THE SOUTH POLE OVERNIGHT. IN REALITY, MAGNETIC POLE SHIFTS ARE GRADUAL PROCESSES THAT CAN TAKE THOUSANDS OF YEARS TO COMPLETE. THE TERM "SUDDEN POLE SHIFT" IS OFTEN CONFLATED WITH RAPID CHANGES IN EARTH'S MAGNETIC FIELD, SUCH AS GEOMAGNETIC JERKS, BUT THESE ARE DISTINCT PHENOMENA.

MYTH 2: POLE SHIFTS CAUSE MASSIVE EARTHQUAKES AND TSUNAMIS

WHILE IT'S TRUE THAT MAGNETIC POLE SHIFTS CAN HAVE GEOLOGICAL CONSEQUENCES, THE IDEA THAT THEY DIRECTLY TRIGGER MASSIVE EARTHQUAKES AND TSUNAMIS IS MISLEADING. POLE SHIFTS ARE NOT SEISMIC EVENTS THEMSELVES BUT CAN INFLUENCE THE EARTH'S GEOPHYSICAL PROCESSES. EARTHQUAKES AND

TSUNAMIS PRIMARILY RESULT FROM THE MOVEMENT OF TECTONIC PLATES, WHICH IS DRIVEN BY DIFFERENT FORCES.

MYTH 3: POLE SHIFTS WILL LEAD TO A COMPLETE REVERSAL OF EARTH'S ROTATION

SOME MYTHS SUGGEST THAT MAGNETIC POLE SHIFTS WOULD CAUSE EARTH'S ROTATION TO REVERSE, LEADING TO CATASTROPHIC UPHEAVAL. IN REALITY, THE EARTH'S ROTATIONAL AXIS AND ITS MAGNETIC AXIS ARE DISTINCT. WHILE MAGNETIC POLE SHIFTS INVOLVE THE REALIGNMENT OF THE MAGNETIC FIELD, THEY DO NOT ALTER THE PLANET'S ROTATION.

MYTH 4: POLE SHIFTS ARE RESPONSIBLE FOR MASS EXTINCTIONS

THERE IS NO DIRECT EVIDENCE LINKING MAGNETIC POLE SHIFTS TO MASS EXTINCTIONS. THE CAUSES OF MAJOR EXTINCTION EVENTS IN EARTH'S HISTORY, SUCH AS THE ASTEROID IMPACT THAT WIPED OUT THE DINOSAURS, ARE MORE COMPLEX AND INVOLVE A COMBINATION OF FACTORS. WHILE

POLE SHIFTS CAN INFLUENCE CLIMATE AND ECOSYSTEMS, ATTRIBUTING MASS EXTINCTIONS SOLELY TO MAGNETIC CHANGES OVERSIMPLIFIES THE ISSUE.

MYTH 5: HUMAN ACTIVITY CAN PREVENT A POLE SHIFT

HUMANS DO NOT HAVE THE CAPACITY TO PREVENT OR CONTROL MAGNETIC POLE SHIFTS. THESE SHIFTS ARE NATURAL PROCESSES DRIVEN BY THE EARTH'S INTERNAL DYNAMICS. WHILE HUMAN ACTIVITIES CAN AFFECT THE PLANET'S MAGNETIC FIELD IN MINOR WAYS, SUCH AS THROUGH MINING AND DRILLING, THEY ARE NOT RESPONSIBLE FOR LARGE-SCALE POLE SHIFTS.

SEPARATING FACT FROM FICTION

DEBUNKING MYTHS AND MISCONCEPTIONS IS A CRUCIAL STEP IN UNDERSTANDING MAGNETIC POLE SHIFTS. HOWEVER, IT'S EQUALLY IMPORTANT TO EMPHASIZE THE SCIENTIFIC FACTS AND FINDINGS RELATED TO THIS PHENOMENON. LET'S

EXPLORE SOME OF THE ESTABLISHED FACTS ABOUT MAGNETIC POLE SHIFTS:

FACT 1: GEOMAGNETIC REVERSALS ARE PART OF EARTH'S HISTORY

GEOLOGICAL RECORDS REVEAL THAT EARTH HAS EXPERIENCED NUMEROUS GEOMAGNETIC REVERSALS THROUGHOUT ITS HISTORY. THESE REVERSALS ARE CHARACTERIZED BY A GRADUAL REALIGNMENT OF THE MAGNETIC POLES. THE LAST REVERSAL, KNOWN AS THE BRUNHES-MATUYAMA REVERSAL, OCCURRED APPROXIMATELY 780,000 YEARS AGO.

FACT 2: MAGNETIC FIELD STRENGTH IS DECREASING

IN RECENT DECADES, SCIENTISTS HAVE OBSERVED A GRADUAL WEAKENING OF EARTH'S MAGNETIC FIELD. THIS WEAKENING TREND IS A SUBJECT OF ONGOING RESEARCH AND DEBATE. WHILE IT DOES NOT NECESSARILY INDICATE AN IMMINENT MAGNETIC POLE SHIFT, IT RAISES QUESTIONS ABOUT THE LONG-TERM STABILITY OF THE FIELD.

FACT 3: MAGNETIC FIELD REVERSALS ARE NOT CATASTROPHIC

CONTRARY TO SOME SENSATIONAL DEPICTIONS, GEOMAGNETIC REVERSALS DO NOT LEAD TO APOCALYPTIC SCENARIOS. EARTH'S MAGNETIC FIELD REMAINS FUNCTIONAL DURING THE REVERSAL PROCESS, ALBEIT WITH CHANGES IN ITS ORIENTATION. THE MAGNETIC SHIELD CONTINUES TO PROTECT THE PLANET FROM SOLAR RADIATION AND COSMIC PARTICLES.

FACT 4: MAGNETIC POLE SHIFTS DO NOT DIRECTLY CAUSE CLIMATE CHANGE

WHILE MAGNETIC POLE SHIFTS CAN INFLUENCE EARTH'S CLIMATE BY ALTERING THE DISTRIBUTION OF SOLAR RADIATION, THEY ARE NOT THE PRIMARY DRIVERS OF CLIMATE CHANGE. LONG-TERM CLIMATE PATTERNS ARE PRIMARILY SHAPED BY FACTORS LIKE GREENHOUSE GAS CONCENTRATIONS, SOLAR VARIABILITY, AND VOLCANIC ACTIVITY.

FACT 5: PREPARING FOR POLE SHIFTS IS ABOUT RESILIENCE

WHILE PREPARING FOR MAGNETIC POLE SHIFTS IS A PRUDENT STEP, IT IS NOT ABOUT FEARING THE UNKNOWN. INSTEAD, IT'S ABOUT FOSTERING RESILIENCE IN THE FACE OF POTENTIAL CHALLENGES. PREPAREDNESS INVOLVES A RANGE OF PRACTICAL MEASURES, FROM SECURING ESSENTIAL SUPPLIES TO DEVELOPING COMMUNITY RESILIENCE STRATEGIES.

PROMOTING CRITICAL THINKING

THE EXPLORATION OF MAGNETIC POLE SHIFTS, LIKE ANY COMPLEX TOPIC, REQUIRES A CRITICAL AND DISCERNING APPROACH. AS WE ENCOUNTER A WEALTH OF INFORMATION, BOTH ACCURATE AND MISLEADING, IT IS INCUMBENT UPON US TO EXERCISE CRITICAL THINKING SKILLS. HERE ARE SOME PRINCIPLES TO KEEP IN MIND:

1. EVALUATE SOURCES

WHEN ASSESSING INFORMATION ABOUT MAGNETIC POLE SHIFTS, CONSIDER THE CREDIBILITY OF THE

SOURCES. RELIABLE SOURCES ARE TYPICALLY GROUNDED IN SCIENTIFIC RESEARCH, PEER-REVIEWED LITERATURE, OR REPUTABLE INSTITUTIONS. BE CAUTIOUS OF SENSATIONALISTIC OR FRINGE SOURCES THAT LACK SCIENTIFIC RIGOR.

2. CROSS-REFERENCE INFORMATION

VERIFY INFORMATION BY CONSULTING MULTIPLE SOURCES. CONSISTENCY AMONG REPUTABLE SOURCES REINFORCES THE ACCURACY OF THE INFORMATION. DISCREPANCIES OR OUTLIER CLAIMS MAY WARRANT FURTHER SCRUTINY.

3. DISTINGUISH BETWEEN FACT AND SPECULATION

DISTINGUISH BETWEEN ESTABLISHED SCIENTIFIC FACTS AND SPECULATIVE THEORIES OR HYPOTHESES. WHILE HYPOTHESES ARE ESSENTIAL FOR SCIENTIFIC EXPLORATION, THEY SHOULD BE CLEARLY IDENTIFIED AS SUCH AND SUBJECT TO EMPIRICAL TESTING.

4. RECOGNIZE COMPLEXITY

ACKNOWLEDGE THE COMPLEXITY OF MAGNETIC POLE SHIFTS AND RELATED PHENOMENA. OVERSIMPLIFIED EXPLANATIONS OR PREDICTIONS OFTEN OVERLOOK THE INTRICATE INTERPLAY OF GEOLOGICAL, GEOMAGNETIC, AND CLIMATIC FACTORS.

5. ENGAGE IN INFORMED DIALOGUE

ENGAGE IN CONSTRUCTIVE AND INFORMED DIALOGUE WITH OTHERS INTERESTED IN THE TOPIC. RESPECTFUL DISCUSSIONS, SUPPORTED BY EVIDENCE AND EXPERTISE, CAN FOSTER A DEEPER UNDERSTANDING OF MAGNETIC POLE SHIFTS.

IN THE CHAPTERS THAT FOLLOW, WE WILL CONTINUE OUR JOURNEY THROUGH THE MULTIFACETED WORLD OF MAGNETIC POLE SHIFTS. WE WILL EXPLORE STRATEGIES FOR PREPARING FOR POTENTIAL DISRUPTIONS, DISCUSS WORST-CASE SCENARIOS, AND CONTEMPLATE THE LONG-TERM FUTURE OF EARTH AND HUMANITY.

CHAPTER 7: PREPARING FOR WORST-CASE SCENARIOS

THE ENIGMA OF MAGNETIC POLE SHIFTS, AS WE'VE COME TO UNDERSTAND, IS A COMPLEX TAPESTRY OF SCIENCE, MYSTICISM, AND PREPAREDNESS. IN THIS CHAPTER, WE CONFRONT THE SOBERING POSSIBILITIES OF WORST-CASE SCENARIOS ASSOCIATED WITH MAGNETIC POLE SHIFTS. WHILE WE HOPE FOR THE BEST, IT IS PRUDENT TO PREPARE FOR THE WORST AND CONTEMPLATE STRATEGIES FOR SURVIVAL AND COMMUNITY RESILIENCE.

WORST-CASE SCENARIOS

MAGNETIC POLE SHIFTS, LIKE MANY NATURAL PHENOMENA, HAVE THE POTENTIAL TO UNLEASH A RANGE OF CHALLENGES AND DISRUPTIONS. WHILE THESE SCENARIOS ARE HYPOTHETICAL, THEY ARE GROUNDED IN SCIENTIFIC UNDERSTANDING AND THE LESSONS OF EARTH'S GEOLOGICAL HISTORY.

SCENARIO 1: GEOMAGNETIC TURMOIL

A MAGNETIC POLE SHIFT CAN INTRODUCE SIGNIFICANT GEOMAGNETIC TURMOIL. DURING THE TRANSITION PERIOD, EARTH'S MAGNETIC FIELD WEAKENS, LEAVING THE PLANET MORE VULNERABLE TO SOLAR RADIATION AND COSMIC PARTICLES. THIS CAN HAVE FAR-REACHING CONSEQUENCES:

- **INCREASED RADIATION EXPOSURE**: HIGHER LEVELS OF RADIATION FROM SPACE MAY POSE HEALTH RISKS TO HUMANS AND ANIMALS.

- **DISRUPTED TECHNOLOGY**: SENSITIVE ELECTRONIC DEVICES, INCLUDING SATELLITES AND COMMUNICATION SYSTEMS, COULD EXPERIENCE MALFUNCTIONS.

- **AURORAS AT UNUSUAL LOCATIONS**: AURORAS, TYPICALLY CONFINED TO POLAR REGIONS, MIGHT BECOME VISIBLE AT LOWER LATITUDES, SIGNALING MAGNETIC INSTABILITY.

SCENARIO 2: CLIMATE DISRUPTIONS

MAGNETIC POLE SHIFTS CAN INFLUENCE CLIMATE PATTERNS, POTENTIALLY LEADING TO:

- **EXTREME WEATHER EVENTS**: SHIFTS IN ATMOSPHERIC CIRCULATION PATTERNS MAY RESULT IN MORE FREQUENT AND SEVERE WEATHER EVENTS, INCLUDING STORMS AND DROUGHTS.

- **SHIFTED HABITABILITY ZONES**: CHANGES IN TEMPERATURE AND PRECIPITATION PATTERNS COULD IMPACT ECOSYSTEMS AND AGRICULTURE.

- **SEA-LEVEL RISE**: DISRUPTED OCEAN CURRENTS MIGHT CONTRIBUTE TO SEA-LEVEL RISE IN CERTAIN REGIONS.

SCENARIO 3: DISRUPTED NAVIGATION

THE RECONFIGURATION OF EARTH'S MAGNETIC FIELD CAN AFFECT NAVIGATION AND ORIENTATION FOR MIGRATORY ANIMALS AND HUMANS WHO RELY ON COMPASSES AND GPS. THE CONSEQUENCES INCLUDE:

- **NAVIGATION CHALLENGES**: MIGRATORY ANIMALS COULD LOSE THEIR ABILITY TO

NAVIGATE ACCURATELY, POTENTIALLY IMPACTING ECOSYSTEMS.

- **TRANSPORTATION DISRUPTIONS**: MARITIME AND AVIATION INDUSTRIES MAY FACE CHALLENGES IN NAVIGATION AND COMMUNICATION.

SCENARIO 4: SOCIETAL INSTABILITY

A MAGNETIC POLE SHIFT'S LONG-TERM EFFECTS ON SOCIETY CAN BE PROFOUND:

- **RESOURCE SCARCITY**: DISRUPTIONS TO AGRICULTURE, WATER SUPPLIES, AND ENERGY PRODUCTION MAY LEAD TO RESOURCE SCARCITY.

- **ECONOMIC CHALLENGES**: DISRUPTED SUPPLY CHAINS AND INFRASTRUCTURE DAMAGE CAN RESULT IN ECONOMIC DOWNTURNS.

- **SOCIAL TENSIONS**: RESOURCE COMPETITION AND MIGRATION COULD LEAD TO SOCIAL TENSIONS AND CONFLICTS.

SCENARIO 5: COMMUNITY RESILIENCE

IN THE FACE OF THESE CHALLENGES, COMMUNITY RESILIENCE BECOMES PARAMOUNT. PREPARING FOR WORST-CASE SCENARIOS INVOLVES A MULTIFACETED APPROACH:

- **LOCAL SELF-SUFFICIENCY**: COMMUNITIES SHOULD AIM TO BECOME SELF-SUFFICIENT IN FOOD, WATER, AND ENERGY PRODUCTION.

- **EMERGENCY RESPONSE**: ROBUST EMERGENCY RESPONSE PLANS SHOULD BE IN PLACE TO ADDRESS IMMEDIATE CRISES.

- **COLLABORATIVE NETWORKS**: COMMUNITIES CAN COLLABORATE TO SHARE RESOURCES AND SUPPORT ONE ANOTHER DURING DIFFICULT TIMES.

THE ROLE OF GOVERNMENT AND ORGANIZATIONS

GOVERNMENTS AND ORGANIZATIONS PLAY PIVOTAL ROLES IN DISASTER PREPAREDNESS AND RESPONSE:

- **EMERGENCY SERVICES**: GOVERNMENTS SHOULD MAINTAIN WELL-EQUIPPED EMERGENCY SERVICES AND SHELTERS.

- **PUBLIC EDUCATION**: PUBLIC EDUCATION PROGRAMS CAN RAISE AWARENESS ABOUT MAGNETIC POLE SHIFTS AND DISASTER PREPAREDNESS.

- **INFRASTRUCTURE RESILIENCE**: CRITICAL INFRASTRUCTURE, SUCH AS POWER GRIDS AND COMMUNICATION SYSTEMS, SHOULD BE DESIGNED TO WITHSTAND DISRUPTIONS.

- **INTERNATIONAL COOPERATION**: AS MAGNETIC POLE SHIFTS ARE GLOBAL EVENTS, INTERNATIONAL COOPERATION IN DISASTER RESPONSE IS ESSENTIAL.

STRATEGIES FOR SURVIVAL

INDIVIDUALS CAN TAKE SEVERAL STEPS TO PREPARE FOR POTENTIAL WORST-CASE SCENARIOS:

- **EMERGENCY KITS**: CREATE EMERGENCY KITS CONTAINING FOOD, WATER, FIRST-AID SUPPLIES, AND ESSENTIAL TOOLS.

- **EVACUATION PLANS**: DEVELOP EVACUATION PLANS AND IDENTIFY SAFE LOCATIONS.

- **COMMUNICATION**: ESTABLISH RELIABLE COMMUNICATION METHODS WITH FAMILY AND COMMUNITY MEMBERS.

- **SKILLS AND TRAINING**: ACQUIRE PRACTICAL SKILLS LIKE FIRST AID, NAVIGATION, AND FOOD PRESERVATION.

- **COMMUNITY ENGAGEMENT**: PARTICIPATE IN LOCAL COMMUNITY PREPAREDNESS EFFORTS.

THE LONG-TERM FUTURE

WHILE CONTEMPLATING WORST-CASE SCENARIOS IS ESSENTIAL FOR PREPAREDNESS, WE MUST ALSO CONSIDER THE LONG-TERM FUTURE. MAGNETIC POLE SHIFTS ARE NATURAL EVENTS IN EARTH'S HISTORY, AND LIFE ON OUR PLANET HAS PERSISTED THROUGH COUNTLESS CHANGES.

AS WE LOOK AHEAD, IT IS WORTH NOTING THAT HUMAN INGENUITY, COOPERATION, AND ADAPTABILITY HAVE ALLOWED US TO OVERCOME EXTRAORDINARY CHALLENGES. BY EMBRACING RESILIENCE, STEWARDSHIP OF OUR PLANET, AND A COMMITMENT TO THE WELL-BEING OF ALL LIVING

BEINGS, WE CAN NAVIGATE THE UNCERTAINTIES OF MAGNETIC POLE SHIFTS AND CONTINUE OUR COLLECTIVE JOURNEY INTO THE FUTURE.

IN THE FINAL CHAPTER OF OUR EXPLORATION, WE WILL REFLECT ON THE PROFOUND SIGNIFICANCE OF MAGNETIC POLE SHIFTS IN THE GRAND TAPESTRY OF EARTH'S HISTORY AND THE EVOLUTION OF LIFE ITSELF.

CHAPTER 7 DIVES INTO WORST-CASE SCENARIOS ASSOCIATED WITH MAGNETIC POLE SHIFTS, EMPHASIZING THE IMPORTANCE OF PREPARATION, COMMUNITY RESILIENCE, AND THE ROLES OF GOVERNMENTS AND ORGANIZATIONS. IT ALSO EXPLORES STRATEGIES FOR SURVIVAL WHILE REMINDING US OF HUMANITY'S ABILITY TO ADAPT AND THRIVE IN THE FACE OF CHALLENGES.

CHAPTER 8: MAGNETIC POLE SHIFTS IN EARTH'S GRAND NARRATIVE

AS WE STAND ON THE PRECIPICE OF THE UNKNOWN, GAZING INTO THE INTRICATE TAPESTRY OF MAGNETIC POLE SHIFTS, IT IS TIME TO REFLECT ON THE PROFOUND SIGNIFICANCE OF THIS PHENOMENON. MAGNETIC POLE SHIFTS ARE NOT ISOLATED EVENTS BUT INTEGRAL CHAPTERS IN EARTH'S GRAND NARRATIVE—A STORY THAT SPANS BILLIONS OF YEARS AND ENCOMPASSES THE EVOLUTION OF LIFE ITSELF.

THE GEOLOGICAL EPIC

THE EARTH'S HISTORY IS A CHRONICLE OF CONSTANT CHANGE—A SYMPHONY OF GEOLOGICAL FORCES, CLIMATIC SHIFTS, AND THE RISE AND FALL OF LIFE FORMS. MAGNETIC POLE SHIFTS ARE BUT ONE STANZA IN THIS EPIC TALE, INTERTWINED WITH THE BROADER GEOLOGICAL NARRATIVE.

GEOLOGICAL RECORD

THE GEOLOGICAL RECORD, INSCRIBED IN THE LAYERS OF ROCK AND SEDIMENT, BEARS WITNESS TO COUNTLESS MAGNETIC POLE SHIFTS THROUGHOUT EARTH'S HISTORY. MAGNETIC

MINERALS, LIKE COMPASS NEEDLES FROZEN IN TIME, RECORD THE SHIFTS IN THE MAGNETIC FIELD. THESE RECORDS TELL US THAT POLE REVERSALS ARE NOT ABERRATIONS BUT RECURRING EVENTS IN EARTH'S STORY.

SHAPING CONTINENTS

MAGNETIC POLE SHIFTS, WHILE GRADUAL ON GEOLOGICAL TIMESCALES, CONTRIBUTE TO THE SHAPING OF CONTINENTS. AS MAGNETIC POLES MIGRATE, CONTINENTS MOVE ALONG WITH THEM. THIS GEOLOGICAL DANCE, KNOWN AS PLATE TECTONICS, HAS SCULPTED EARTH'S SURFACE OVER EONS, GIVING RISE TO MOUNTAIN RANGES, OCEAN BASINS, AND THE DIVERSE LANDSCAPES WE SEE TODAY.

CLIMATE CHANGE AND EVOLUTION

MAGNETIC POLE SHIFTS HAVE ALSO PLAYED A ROLE IN CLIMATE CHANGE AND EVOLUTION. CHANGES IN EARTH'S MAGNETIC FIELD INFLUENCE THE DISTRIBUTION OF SOLAR RADIATION AND COSMIC PARTICLES, WHICH, IN TURN, IMPACT

CLIMATE PATTERNS. THESE SHIFTS HAVE SPURRED ADAPTATIONS AND EVOLUTIONARY CHANGES IN LIVING ORGANISMS, FROM ANCIENT MICROBES TO MODERN HUMANS.

THE COSMIC CONNECTION

BEYOND EARTH'S CONFINES, MAGNETIC POLE SHIFTS ARE PART OF A BROADER COSMIC TAPESTRY—A SYMPHONY OF CELESTIAL EVENTS THAT SHAPE OUR PLANET'S DESTINY.

SOLAR INFLUENCE

THE SUN, OUR CELESTIAL NEIGHBOR, EXERTS A PROFOUND INFLUENCE ON EARTH'S MAGNETIC FIELD. SOLAR ACTIVITY, CHARACTERIZED BY THE SUN'S MAGNETIC CYCLES, CAN INTERACT WITH EARTH'S MAGNETIC FIELD, LEADING TO GEOMAGNETIC DISTURBANCES. UNDERSTANDING THESE INTERACTIONS IS CRUCIAL FOR PREDICTING AND PREPARING FOR MAGNETIC POLE SHIFTS.

GALACTIC DYNAMICS

ON AN EVEN GRANDER SCALE, EARTH'S MAGNETIC FIELD IS INFLUENCED BY THE DYNAMICS OF OUR

MILKY WAY GALAXY. AS OUR SOLAR SYSTEM JOURNEYS THROUGH THE GALAXY, IT ENCOUNTERS COSMIC RAYS AND MAGNETIC FIELDS FROM OTHER CELESTIAL BODIES. THESE INTERACTIONS CONTRIBUTE TO THE EVER-EVOLVING NATURE OF EARTH'S MAGNETIC FIELD.

THE HUMAN STORY

IN THE GRAND NARRATIVE OF EARTH'S HISTORY, HUMANITY OCCUPIES BUT A BRIEF CHAPTER—A CHAPTER MARKED BY INNOVATION, EXPLORATION, AND THE QUEST FOR UNDERSTANDING. MAGNETIC POLE SHIFTS POSE UNIQUE CHALLENGES AND OPPORTUNITIES FOR OUR SPECIES.

THE QUEST FOR KNOWLEDGE

AS HUMANS, WE HAVE EMBARKED ON A RELENTLESS QUEST TO UNRAVEL THE MYSTERIES OF OUR PLANET AND THE COSMOS. SCIENTIFIC INQUIRY INTO MAGNETIC POLE SHIFTS EXEMPLIFIES OUR INNATE CURIOSITY AND THIRST FOR KNOWLEDGE. THROUGH RESEARCH,

OBSERVATION, AND COLLABORATION, WE CONTINUE TO EXPAND OUR UNDERSTANDING OF THIS PHENOMENON.

CHALLENGES AND RESILIENCE

MAGNETIC POLE SHIFTS CHALLENGE OUR ADAPTABILITY AND RESILIENCE. THESE EVENTS TEST OUR CAPACITY TO COPE WITH DISRUPTIONS TO TECHNOLOGY, INFRASTRUCTURE, AND ECOSYSTEMS. YET, IN THE FACE OF ADVERSITY, HUMAN INGENUITY AND THE SPIRIT OF COOPERATION HAVE ALLOWED US TO NAVIGATE CRISES WITH TENACITY AND RESOLVE.

STEWARDSHIP OF EARTH

PERHAPS THE MOST PROFOUND LESSON MAGNETIC POLE SHIFTS OFFER IS THAT OF STEWARDSHIP. OUR ACTIONS AS STEWARDS OF THE PLANET HAVE FAR-REACHING CONSEQUENCES. HUMAN ACTIVITIES, SUCH AS DEFORESTATION, POLLUTION, AND CLIMATE CHANGE, CAN AMPLIFY THE CHALLENGES POSED BY MAGNETIC POLE SHIFTS. EMBRACING RESPONSIBLE STEWARDSHIP AND

SUSTAINABILITY IS ESSENTIAL FOR SAFEGUARDING OUR FUTURE.

THE TAPESTRY UNFOLDS

AS WE CONCLUDE OUR EXPLORATION OF MAGNETIC POLE SHIFTS, WE ARE REMINDED THAT EARTH'S STORY IS AN ONGOING NARRATIVE—ONE IN WHICH WE ALL PLAY A PART. THE CHAPTERS OF THIS STORY ARE WRITTEN NOT IN ISOLATION BUT IN CONCERT WITH THE NATURAL WORLD AND THE COSMOS.

A CALL TO ACTION

MAGNETIC POLE SHIFTS, WHILE SHROUDED IN MYSTERY, SERVE AS A CALL TO ACTION. THEY BECKON US TO CULTIVATE A DEEP REVERENCE FOR THE PLANET THAT SUSTAINS US AND TO FORGE A HARMONIOUS RELATIONSHIP WITH THE EARTH'S MAGNETIC HEARTBEAT.

COLLABORATION AND UNITY

IN THE GRAND NARRATIVE OF EARTH'S HISTORY, COLLABORATION AND UNITY ARE THE THREADS THAT BIND US. MAGNETIC POLE SHIFTS KNOW NO

BORDERS OR DIVISIONS. THEY UNDERSCORE OUR INTERCONNECTEDNESS AS A GLOBAL COMMUNITY, EMPHASIZING THE IMPORTANCE OF WORKING TOGETHER TO CONFRONT CHALLENGES AND EMBRACE OPPORTUNITIES.

A CONTINUATION OF WONDER

AS WE TURN THE PAGE ON THIS CHAPTER OF EXPLORATION, LET US CARRY FORWARD THE WONDER AND CURIOSITY THAT HAVE GUIDED US. MAGNETIC POLE SHIFTS ARE BUT ONE ENIGMA IN THE VAST COSMOS OF UNANSWERED QUESTIONS. OUR JOURNEY IS FAR FROM OVER, AND THE TAPESTRY OF EARTH'S STORY CONTINUES TO UNFOLD.

IN CLOSING, LET US EMBRACE THE LESSONS OF MAGNETIC POLE SHIFTS—A TESTAMENT TO THE ENDURING SPIRIT OF INQUIRY, THE POWER OF ADAPTATION, AND THE AWE-INSPIRING COMPLEXITY OF OUR WORLD. AS WE GAZE INTO THE HORIZON OF THE UNKNOWN, LET US DO SO WITH HEARTS FULL OF WONDER, MINDS BRIMMING

WITH CURIOSITY, AND A DEEP SENSE OF RESPONSIBILITY FOR THE FUTURE OF OUR PLANET.

THE JOURNEY OF UNDERSTANDING IS UNENDING, AND THE MAGNETIC POLE SHIFTS, WITH ALL THEIR ENIGMATIC BEAUTY, ARE BUT A SINGLE CHAPTER IN THE BOUNDLESS STORY OF EARTH.

CHAPTER 9: INTO THE FUTURE

AS WE CONCLUDE OUR EXPLORATION OF MAGNETIC POLE SHIFTS, WE FIND OURSELVES AT THE CROSSROADS OF KNOWLEDGE, PREPAREDNESS, AND WONDER. THE JOURNEY WE'VE UNDERTAKEN HAS SHED LIGHT ON THE MULTIFACETED NATURE OF THIS PHENOMENON, FROM ITS SCIENTIFIC UNDERPINNINGS TO ITS MYSTIC PERSPECTIVES, FROM THE MYTHS AND MISCONCEPTIONS THAT SHROUD IT TO THE STRATEGIES FOR SURVIVAL AND RESILIENCE.

A CONTINUAL QUEST FOR UNDERSTANDING

THE STUDY OF MAGNETIC POLE SHIFTS IS AN ONGOING, DYNAMIC ENDEAVOR. SCIENTISTS AND RESEARCHERS AROUND THE WORLD CONTINUE TO PROBE THE MYSTERIES OF EARTH'S MAGNETIC FIELD, SEEKING ANSWERS TO QUESTIONS THAT HAVE CAPTIVATED HUMAN CURIOSITY FOR CENTURIES.

ADVANCEMENTS IN SCIENCE

SCIENTIFIC ADVANCEMENTS IN FIELDS SUCH AS GEOMAGNETISM, GEOPHYSICS, AND SPACE WEATHER PREDICTION ARE INSTRUMENTAL IN EXPANDING OUR UNDERSTANDING OF MAGNETIC POLE SHIFTS. NEW TECHNOLOGIES, SATELLITE MISSIONS, AND INTERDISCIPLINARY COLLABORATIONS ARE OPENING DOORS TO FRESH INSIGHTS.

THE ROLE OF CITIZEN SCIENCE

CITIZEN SCIENTISTS ALSO PLAY A VITAL ROLE IN MONITORING AND STUDYING MAGNETIC POLE SHIFTS. AMATEUR ASTRONOMERS, GEOLOGY ENTHUSIASTS, AND DEDICATED INDIVIDUALS

CONTRIBUTE OBSERVATIONS AND DATA, ENRICHING THE COLLECTIVE KNOWLEDGE BASE.

BUILDING RESILIENCE AND PREPAREDNESS

IN THE FACE OF UNCERTAINTY, PREPAREDNESS REMAINS A CORNERSTONE OF RESILIENCE. WHILE THE SPECIFICS OF MAGNETIC POLE SHIFTS MAY ELUDE PRECISE PREDICTION, THE PRINCIPLES OF READINESS APPLY UNIVERSALLY.

COMMUNITY PREPAREDNESS

COMMUNITIES WORLDWIDE ARE STRENGTHENING THEIR PREPAREDNESS EFFORTS. THEY ARE COLLABORATING, SHARING KNOWLEDGE, AND DEVELOPING STRATEGIES TO ENSURE THE WELL-BEING OF THEIR MEMBERS IN THE EVENT OF DISRUPTIONS.

ENVIRONMENTAL STEWARDSHIP

ENVIRONMENTAL STEWARDSHIP AND SUSTAINABILITY ARE ESSENTIAL ELEMENTS OF RESILIENCE. RECOGNIZING THE INTERCONNECTEDNESS OF EARTH'S SYSTEMS, INDIVIDUALS AND COMMUNITIES ARE EMBRACING

RESPONSIBLE PRACTICES TO PROTECT THE ENVIRONMENT.

EMBRACING THE UNKNOWN

MAGNETIC POLE SHIFTS SERVE AS A REMINDER THAT THE UNIVERSE IS VAST, ENIGMATIC, AND EVER-EVOLVING. THE UNKNOWN BECKONS US WITH ITS MYSTERIES, PROMPTING US TO EMBRACE CURIOSITY AND EXPLORATION.

EXPANDING HORIZONS

AS OUR UNDERSTANDING OF MAGNETIC POLE SHIFTS DEEPENS, IT OPENS DOORS TO BROADER QUESTIONS ABOUT THE COSMOS. WE CONTEMPLATE THE ROLE OF MAGNETIC FIELDS IN CELESTIAL BODIES, THE POTENTIAL FOR LIFE BEYOND EARTH, AND THE INTERCONNECTEDNESS OF THE UNIVERSE.

A CALL TO UNITY

IN THE GRAND SCHEME OF THE COSMOS, WE ARE BUT A PALE BLUE DOT—A FRAGILE OASIS IN THE VASTNESS OF SPACE. MAGNETIC POLE SHIFTS UNDERSCORE OUR COMMON HUMANITY AND THE

SHARED RESPONSIBILITY TO SAFEGUARD OUR PLANET.

THE ENDLESS WONDER

THE STORY OF MAGNETIC POLE SHIFTS, LIKE THE STORY OF EARTH ITSELF, IS A TALE OF WONDER—A TESTAMENT TO THE HUMAN SPIRIT'S RELENTLESS QUEST FOR KNOWLEDGE AND THE PROFOUND BEAUTY OF THE NATURAL WORLD.

THE WONDER OF DISCOVERY

AS WE JOURNEY FORWARD, LET US CARRY THE WONDER OF DISCOVERY WITH US. LET US REMAIN OPEN TO THE MYSTERIES THAT SURROUND US AND THE REVELATIONS THAT AWAIT OUR INQUIRY.

A SHARED VISION

IN THE SPIRIT OF SHARED VISION, LET US WORK TOGETHER TO NURTURE A WORLD WHERE SCIENCE, MYSTICISM, PREPAREDNESS, AND WONDER COEXIST HARMONIOUSLY—A WORLD WHERE WE RECOGNIZE OUR INTERCONNECTEDNESS WITH THE COSMOS AND OUR PROFOUND RESPONSIBILITY TO THE PLANET WE CALL HOME.

IN CLOSING, THE EXPLORATION OF MAGNETIC POLE SHIFTS IS A TESTAMENT TO THE ENDURING HUMAN SPIRIT—AN EXPLORATION THAT TRANSCENDS BORDERS, DIVISIONS, AND DISCIPLINES. AS WE VENTURE INTO THE FUTURE, MAY WE DO SO WITH HEARTS FULL OF WONDER AND MINDS ABLAZE WITH CURIOSITY, EVER READY TO EMBRACE THE MYSTERIES THAT LIE AHEAD.

THE JOURNEY CONTINUES, AND THE MAGNETIC POLE SHIFTS REMAIN AN ENDURING ENIGMA IN THE GRAND TAPESTRY OF EARTH'S HISTORY AND THE COSMOS ITSELF.

CONCLUSION: NAVIGATING THE MAGNETIC PUZZLE - KEY TAKEAWAYS AND ACTIONS

OUR JOURNEY THROUGH THE FASCINATING WORLD OF MAGNETIC POLE SHIFTS HAS BEEN ONE OF PROFOUND DISCOVERY AND CONTEMPLATION. FROM THE SCIENTIFIC INTRICACIES TO THE MYSTIC PERSPECTIVES, FROM DEBUNKING MYTHS TO EMBRACING PREPAREDNESS, WE'VE NAVIGATED THIS ENIGMATIC PUZZLE WITH CURIOSITY AND

PURPOSE. NOW, AS WE CONCLUDE OUR EXPLORATION, IT'S TIME TO DISTILL THE KEY TAKEAWAYS AND CHART A COURSE OF ACTION FOR A FUTURE MARKED BY RESILIENCE, STEWARDSHIP, AND WONDER.

KEY TAKEAWAYS

1. MAGNETIC POLE SHIFTS ARE INTRINSIC TO EARTH'S HISTORY

THROUGHOUT EARTH'S VAST HISTORY, MAGNETIC POLE SHIFTS HAVE BEEN RECURRING PHENOMENA. GEOLOGICAL RECORDS REVEAL A TAPESTRY OF REVERSALS, PROVIDING INSIGHTS INTO THE DYNAMIC NATURE OF OUR PLANET. UNDERSTANDING THAT THESE SHIFTS ARE A NATURAL PART OF EARTH'S STORY IS THE FIRST STEP IN DEMYSTIFYING THEM.

2. GRADUAL AND ONGOING TRANSFORMATION

MAGNETIC POLE SHIFTS ARE NOT SUDDEN CATACLYSMS BUT GRADUAL AND ONGOING PROCESSES. THEY OCCUR OVER THOUSANDS OF YEARS, MARKED BY FLUCTUATIONS AND

GEOMAGNETIC EXCURSIONS RATHER THAN ABRUPT REVERSALS. THIS GRADUALISM ALLOWS FOR ADAPTATION AND RESILIENCE.

3. DIVERSE PERSPECTIVES ILLUMINATE THE PHENOMENON

THE STUDY OF MAGNETIC POLE SHIFTS DRAWS FROM A MULTITUDE OF DISCIPLINES AND PERSPECTIVES. WHILE THE SCIENTIFIC EXPLORATION UNVEILS THE UNDERLYING MECHANISMS, MYSTIC VIEWPOINTS OFFER METAPHYSICAL INSIGHTS. ACKNOWLEDGING THE DIVERSITY OF PERSPECTIVES ENRICHES OUR UNDERSTANDING OF THIS COMPLEX PHENOMENON.

4. DEBUNKING MYTHS AND MISCONCEPTIONS

SEPARATING FACT FROM FICTION IS CRUCIAL IN COMPREHENDING MAGNETIC POLE SHIFTS. MYTHS AND MISCONCEPTIONS, OFTEN FUELED BY SENSATIONALISM, CAN CLOUD OUR JUDGMENT AND HINDER PREPAREDNESS EFFORTS. CRITICAL THINKING AND RELIABLE SOURCES ARE OUR ALLIES IN THIS ENDEAVOR.

5. PREPAREDNESS IS AN ACT OF RESILIENCE

PREPAREDNESS FOR MAGNETIC POLE SHIFTS AND OTHER DISASTERS IS A RESPONSIBLE AND PRUDENT COURSE OF ACTION. IT INVOLVES A MULTIFACETED APPROACH ENCOMPASSING FOOD AND WATER SECURITY, SHELTER AND SURVIVAL GEAR, ENERGY ALTERNATIVES, SECURITY MEASURES, SKILLS AND TRAINING, AND COMMUNITY NETWORKING. PREPAREDNESS FOSTERS RESILIENCE IN THE FACE OF UNCERTAINTY.

6. GOVERNMENT AND ORGANIZATIONAL ROLES

GOVERNMENT AGENCIES LIKE FEMA AND EMERGENCY DISASTER SPECIALISTS PLAY PIVOTAL ROLES IN DISASTER PREPAREDNESS AND RESPONSE. THEIR RESPONSIBILITIES INCLUDE COORDINATION, MITIGATION, RECOVERY ASSISTANCE, AND PUBLIC EDUCATION. COLLABORATIVE EFFORTS BETWEEN GOVERNMENTS, ORGANIZATIONS, AND

COMMUNITIES ARE ESSENTIAL FOR COMPREHENSIVE PREPAREDNESS.

7. SCIENCE AND EXPLORATION PERSIST

THE QUEST FOR UNDERSTANDING MAGNETIC POLE SHIFTS IS AN ONGOING ENDEAVOR. SCIENTIFIC ADVANCEMENTS, INTERDISCIPLINARY COLLABORATIONS, AND THE CONTRIBUTIONS OF CITIZEN SCIENTISTS CONTINUE TO EXPAND OUR KNOWLEDGE. OUR THIRST FOR KNOWLEDGE AND EXPLORATION KNOWS NO BOUNDS.

8. RESILIENCE AND STEWARDSHIP

IN THE GRAND NARRATIVE OF EARTH'S HISTORY, RESILIENCE AND STEWARDSHIP EMERGE AS GUIDING PRINCIPLES. BUILDING RESILIENCE AT THE INDIVIDUAL AND COMMUNITY LEVELS IS A TESTAMENT TO HUMAN ADAPTABILITY AND DETERMINATION. RESPONSIBLE STEWARDSHIP OF THE ENVIRONMENT IS ESSENTIAL TO MITIGATE THE IMPACT OF HUMAN ACTIVITIES ON MAGNETIC POLE SHIFTS AND BROADER ECOLOGICAL CHALLENGES.

9. EMBRACING WONDER AND UNITY

MAGNETIC POLE SHIFTS, LIKE THE COSMOS ITSELF, EVOKE A SENSE OF WONDER AND UNITY. THEY REMIND US OF OUR INTERCONNECTEDNESS AS A GLOBAL COMMUNITY AND OUR SHARED RESPONSIBILITY FOR THE PLANET. THE MYSTERIES OF THE COSMOS CALL UPON US TO REMAIN OPEN TO DISCOVERY AND AWE.

ACTIONS FOR THE FUTURE

OUR EXPLORATION OF MAGNETIC POLE SHIFTS HAS LAID THE GROUNDWORK FOR INFORMED ACTIONS IN THE FACE OF UNCERTAINTY. AS WE MOVE INTO THE FUTURE, LET US CONSIDER THE FOLLOWING ACTIONS:

1. FOSTER SCIENCE AND EDUCATION

. SUPPORT SCIENTIFIC RESEARCH INTO GEOMAGNETISM AND MAGNETIC POLE SHIFTS.

. ADVOCATE FOR ROBUST EDUCATIONAL PROGRAMS THAT TEACH STUDENTS ABOUT EARTH'S MAGNETIC FIELD AND THE IMPORTANCE OF PREPAREDNESS.

2. PROMOTE PREPAREDNESS

- DEVELOP PERSONAL AND COMMUNITY EMERGENCY PREPAREDNESS PLANS.

- ENGAGE IN TRAINING AND ACQUIRE SKILLS THAT ENHANCE RESILIENCE IN TIMES OF CRISIS.

- FOSTER A CULTURE OF PREPAREDNESS THAT EXTENDS TO FRIENDS, FAMILY, AND NEIGHBORS.

3. ADVOCATE FOR ENVIRONMENTAL STEWARDSHIP

- EMBRACE SUSTAINABLE PRACTICES THAT REDUCE ENVIRONMENTAL IMPACT.

- ADVOCATE FOR POLICIES THAT ADDRESS CLIMATE CHANGE, DEFORESTATION, AND POLLUTION.

- SUPPORT ORGANIZATIONS AND INITIATIVES FOCUSED ON ENVIRONMENTAL PRESERVATION.

4. ENCOURAGE INTERDISCIPLINARY COLLABORATION

- PROMOTE COLLABORATION BETWEEN SCIENTIFIC DISCIPLINES TO GAIN A HOLISTIC UNDERSTANDING OF MAGNETIC POLE SHIFTS.

- ENGAGE WITH CITIZEN SCIENCE PROJECTS THAT ALLOW INDIVIDUALS TO CONTRIBUTE TO RESEARCH EFFORTS.

5. STRENGTHEN COMMUNITY RESILIENCE

- ESTABLISH OR JOIN LOCAL PREPAREDNESS NETWORKS AND ORGANIZATIONS.

- SHARE KNOWLEDGE AND RESOURCES WITHIN YOUR COMMUNITY TO ENHANCE COLLECTIVE RESILIENCE.

- ENGAGE IN DIALOGUE AND COLLABORATION WITH LOCAL GOVERNMENTS AND EMERGENCY SERVICES.

6. INSPIRE WONDER AND CURIOSITY

- CULTIVATE A SENSE OF WONDER ABOUT THE NATURAL WORLD AND THE COSMOS.

- ENCOURAGE CURIOSITY AND EXPLORATION IN YOUNG MINDS, NURTURING FUTURE SCIENTISTS AND THINKERS.

- SHARE THE BEAUTY OF SCIENTIFIC DISCOVERIES AND THE MYSTERIES OF MAGNETIC POLE SHIFTS WITH OTHERS.

7. ADVOCATE FOR UNITY

- PROMOTE UNITY AND COLLABORATION AMONG NATIONS, RECOGNIZING THAT MAGNETIC POLE SHIFTS ARE GLOBAL PHENOMENA.

- ADVOCATE FOR INTERNATIONAL COOPERATION IN DISASTER RESPONSE AND CLIMATE CHANGE MITIGATION.

- SUPPORT ORGANIZATIONS WORKING TOWARDS GLOBAL UNITY AND SUSTAINABILITY.

IN CLOSING

AS WE BRING OUR JOURNEY THROUGH THE MAGNETIC PUZZLE TO A CLOSE, WE ARE REMINDED THAT THE QUEST FOR UNDERSTANDING IS UNENDING. THE ENIGMA OF MAGNETIC POLE

SHIFTS SERVES AS A BEACON, ILLUMINATING OUR PATH FORWARD—A PATH MARKED BY RESILIENCE, STEWARDSHIP, AND WONDER.

IN THE GRAND NARRATIVE OF EARTH'S HISTORY, WE ARE BUT A SINGLE CHAPTER—A FLEETING MOMENT IN THE VAST EXPANSE OF TIME. YET, OUR ACTIONS, OUR CURIOSITY, AND OUR COMMITMENT TO THE WELL-BEING OF OUR PLANET CAN ECHO THROUGH THE AGES.

THE MAGNETIC POLE SHIFTS ARE NOT AN END BUT A CONTINUATION OF THE STORY—A STORY THAT INVITES US TO EXPLORE, TO PREPARE, TO WONDER, AND TO UNITE. IN THE FACE OF THE UNKNOWN, MAY WE MARCH FORWARD WITH UNWAVERING DETERMINATION, GUIDED BY THE MAGNETIC PULSE OF CURIOSITY THAT BEATS WITHIN US ALL.

DAVID HOLMAN